PARENT 4 LIFE

Roots and Wings

DR LAURA L. FREEMAN

ISBN: 1492861898
ISBN 13: 9781492861898
Library of Congress Control Number: 2013919742
CreateSpace Independent Publishing Platform
North Charleston, South Carolina

I want to dedicate this book to my five wonderful children:
Lisa, Scott, Jeff, Michelle, and Christine.
Through each of you, I have learned so much about life
and even more about myself.
My hope is that I have given you the roots
and wings you needed and that you
will do the same for your own children.
I love you all very much!

Table of Contents

Parent4Life

_____

Introduction: *Roots and Wings*

THE FIRST TIME I CONSCIOUSLY thought about my role as a parent and the immense responsibility of that role, I was sitting at my oldest child's high school graduation. I was scared, worried, and under the effects of radiation and chemotherapy, after having received a diagnosis of cancer one month prior. Because I am the mother of five children, you would think that the idea of a parent's responsibility would have crossed my mind in earlier years, but one does not usually think about death or the uncertainty of life until it becomes personal. During my weekly visits to the chemo lab, being pumped full of "good" poison, my life as a parent became my only thought. I worried about what the immediate future held for me and, most importantly, for my children. When I was diagnosed with cancer, I kept thinking how unfair it was and wondered what I should do to make sure my children would be taken care of if something were to happen to me. Of course, this would have crossed any parent's mind in that situation, but what's most significant is that it took a life-threatening illness for me to ask myself what impact I had had on my children up to that point in their lives. Could

I have done more to positively impact them? And, more critically, how could I be a better parent from that day forward?

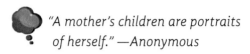 *"A mother's children are portraits of herself." —Anonymous*

Parenting is difficult, rewarding, and scary, and sometimes even words can't explain the broad spectrum of emotions a parent experiences. In this ever-changing world, we must all ask ourselves what we can do to positively impact children's lives and help prepare them for the future. As a mother, I must be able to focus on the priorities that are most important in my child's development.

Before I had children, friends and family members would always tell me that you could never prepare enough for becoming a parent. As I didn't yet have children, that didn't make much sense to me. I even had one friend who had meticulously planned out the best time for her and her husband to have children—financial goals to be met, the purchase of a specific car and house of adequate size, best geographic location to raise a child, etc. Needless to say, that all went out the window when her birth control failed and the pregnancy test came back positive!

I am not sure anybody can really be fully prepared when having a child. Many years ago there was a movie called Sliding Doors. The first few minutes depict a woman waiting to board a subway car. The doors slide open and she gets on the subway car. Then a parallel scene shows the same woman at the same station, only this time the doors close before she can get on. From then on the movie shows the consequences of her getting onto that subway car or not—thus the title of the movie, Sliding Doors. As I look back on my life, there have been so many times I have wondered—if I had taken an alternate path, how different would my life be today? I am sure you can relate to this and think about the choices you have made in your own life. So because of the particular sliding door I chose to walk through, I have been blessed with five children: Lisa, Scott, Jeff, Michelle, and Christine. I never really planned or prepared myself for the role of being a parent. The span between my oldest and youngest is seven years, and I hit the "daily double" with twins in the middle. I have had the opportunity to experience many things as a parent of five children. You might think that it must have gotten easier with each one, sometimes yes and other times no. Whether raising one child or many, it's a hard job.

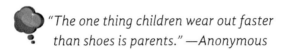 *"The one thing children wear out faster than shoes is parents." —Anonymous*

In psychology, there is a term called a "life-changing event," meaning that someone experiences an event that literally transforms the course of his or her life. My experience with cancer was a life-changing event for me. Becoming a parent is technically considered a life-changing event too, but it's a no-return, no-exchange, no-quit event that differs from other events like moving or changing jobs. I have heard people comment that when you have a baby, it will change your life for the next eighteen years. I beg to differ: it's a life-changing event that does not stop when a child turns eighteen.

When I was growing up, my mother had a small piece of art in her bedroom. It looked like a framed postcard. I could read the words, but I never understood what they meant until much later in my life. It said, "There are two things in life you give your children: roots and wings." This came from a poem that was written from a child's perspective. Dr. Denis Waitley, author of The

Psychology of Success and other books, elaborates on this idea of roots and wings in the following poem:

> *If I had two wishes, I know what they would be:*
> *I'd wish for roots to cling to, and wings to set me free.*
>
> *Roots of inner values, like rings within a tree,*
> *And wings of independence, to seek my destiny.*
>
> *Roots to hold forever to keep me safe and strong,*
> *To let me know you love me, when I've done something wrong.*
>
> *To show me by example, and help me learn to choose,*
> *To take those actions every day, to win instead of lose.*
>
> *Just be there when I need you, to tell me it's all right,*
> *To face my fear of falling when I test my wings in flight.*
>
> *Don't make my life too easy; it's better if I try*
> *And fail and get back up myself, so I can learn to fly.*
>
> *If I had two wishes, and two were all I had,*
> *And they could just be granted, by my mom and dad*
>
> *I wouldn't ask for money, or any store-bought things,*
> *The greatest gifts I'd ask for are simply roots and wings.*

I think both of my parents lived by that saying, giving me a foundation of roots that are embedded forever and wings that allowed me to explore my life—not always in the ways they might have wanted, but in the ways I needed. How simple it sounds to give my children roots and wings, but sometimes it has been so difficult to do.

So what does it mean to give your children roots and wings? As a parent, roots and wings should become tangible, something you can see and feel in your own behavior. Roots are very much like those of a tree: some trees have deep roots, while others have shallow roots. Developing deep roots for a child involves being a role model for those things that are most important for the child's well-being. Strong roots develop good self-esteem; are grounded in doing what is right and finding comfort in coming home; and provide nourishment for the body and mind, a close attachment, and the warmth of being part of a family.

Wings are developed by teaching your children to make their own decisions, to seek out new opportunities, and to be able to pick up the pieces when something doesn't work out. Wings provide children the opportunity to soar and seek out who they are and what their interests are. A parent can actually see children's wings after accomplishments and in the excitement in their eyes when they find their passions. Wings can be scary, especially for the parent, but they also provide a feeling of gratitude in seeing children soar. Giving your children roots and wings doesn't happen overnight and is not without tears. Taking one step and one day at a time, you can build strong roots for your children and the wings for them to soar on into adulthood and beyond.

 "It will be gone before you know it. The fingerprints on the wall appear higher and higher. Then suddenly disappear." —Anonymous

According to *Webster's Dictionary*, the definition of "mysterious" is "exciting wonder, curiosity, or surprise while baffling efforts to comprehend or identify." Parenting is rarely described as being mysterious, but in some ways it is. There are so many unknowns at the time of having a child: What will I name the baby? Who will the child look like? Will he or she be a good baby and sleep all night? But those are the easy mysteries; they get much more difficult once that child is born. Why is my baby crying so much? Why is my child having a meltdown in the middle of the store? Why is she saying she hates me (and yes, it does happen!)? From a parent's viewpoint, children can be a mystery!

In this book, when I talk about being a parent, I'm using a very broad definition. A parent can be a biological mother or father, but the term can encompass much more than that, especially in today's world. There are single parents and same-sex couples raising children. I also consider those who are raising a stepchild, or grandparents participating in a child's life, as having parental responsibilities. It's all about the impact, the accountability, and the legacy that reside in the parental role. There are many times that parents don't understand the responsibilities that come with parenting. And it's not an easy task, so let's stop pretending it is. Parenting is a continuous balance; it's about learning to be the best parent possible in order to provide the two things all children need: roots and wings. Parenting does not stop when a child reaches the age of eighteen. It is a labor of love and support that lasts a lifetime.

As I have already mentioned, the premise of this book is simple: roots and wings. After raising my five children, achieving my doctorate in psychology, and many years of parenting, I challenge you to think about the impact you have on your children's lives and how to make it the best possible experience for both you and them. While reading this book, have some good laughs (there are many funny, true stories) and shed some tears. You may like or

dislike some of my suggestions and activities, but it's all about being a Parent4Life—and taking the responsibility to do so. So read,
laugh, cry, and most of all, enjoy!

> *Note: Purple is my favorite color, so embedded in
> each chapter you will find three purple sidebars.
> One is a personal quote that I like; one is a funny,
> true story; and one is a Parent4Life activity that I
> hope you will use.*

Parent4Life Lesson One
_____

Prioritize before You Drive Yourself Crazy!

PROFESSIONALLY, I HAVE WORKED MANY years with various companies as an industrial and organizational psychologist. If you are unfamiliar with this field, as many are, it is similar to a clinical psychologist, but it focuses on businesses and the behaviors of employees. One area of expertise is coaching employees in how to prioritize their work—teaching employees how to decide what is critically important to accomplish today, this week, and this month. Some people can do it very well; others struggle because they don't have a sifting process that moves different items to the top as their priorities change in the business. Sometimes, not having this skill can derail an employee's career.

Similarly, as a parent, you must be able to understand and acknowledge your priorities. This is somewhat individual for every parent, with the exception of child endangerment. We as parents must decide where we will hold our children accountable and what our priorities are. Everything can't be critical all the time! Like I said, it's easy to prioritize when a child puts him- or herself in danger—crossing the street without an adult, playing with a lighter, etc. Safety for your child is a priority, and you must lay down rules or foundational roots around safety precautions. These foundational roots should be strong and should not bend. But we parents have so many priorities, so many battles to choose. We must decide what our children do that really bothers us and what things we can live with. However, sometimes parents begin to assume everything is top priority, and this is unhealthy. Everything cannot be a priority all the time this will lead to confusion and unwanted stress for child and parent.

Like I mentioned in the introduction, I will use lots of personal stories to illustrate my advice, so it's OK to laugh. I know you are laughing with me, not at me!

I have never been a clotheshorse or enjoyed shopping just for fun. But when my first child, Lisa, was born, I did enjoy buying some frilly girl clothes for my daughter. I wanted to make sure she had cute, matching booties and bows with her outfits. Pregnancy number two brought my twins, Scott and Jeff, and even though I didn't feel that the clothes were as cute, I did have fun with their matching outfits! I would usually buy the same outfit, but Scott would have one in red and Jeff would have it in blue. It wasn't until the twins went to preschool that I found out Jeff was color-blind. Luckily, Jeff was dressed in one of the few colors he could see—blue! Even today, Jeff sees most colors as brown, so I guess he always thought his brother wore brown 24/7! In addition, if I got really creative, I would match all three children in the same patterned outfits. It was cute, but I'm not sure it was worth the effort of shopping, making sure all the clothes were clean and pressed, and then dressing three kids!

When child number four, Michelle, was born, I still had some hand-me-downs from my first daughter, but I bought Michelle more dresses, thinking I would really spend the time with the dress, booties, and bows in her hair (except she didn't have any hair until she was eighteen months old!). As you can imagine, with three older children who were ages three and five, my fascination with playing dress-up went out the window very quickly. It was not until child number five, Christine, was born that I came to the realization that having all matching outfits or coordinating pants, shirts, shoes, and socks was really not that important to me. In fact, I didn't have enough strength or hours in a day to worry about what each of the children was wearing to school or daycare. It was more important that I had five lunches made and that they had homework completed before the morning madness started. I decided my foundational root with regards to clothes was that each child had to have clean clothes on, but they didn't have to match with anything or anyone else. It was amusing to watch Lisa trying to dress Michelle and Christine in whatever, and because Jeff didn't see most colors, he kept asking his siblings what color his clothes were. The morning rush became rather entertaining when I let go of the need to have perfection among outfits. It was no longer my priority. As my youngest daughter, Christine, will tell you, coupled with the evidence of pictures (yes, I took pictures of them dressed in who-knows-what), Christine became known as the "princess of mismatch." But you know what? My stress level was much lower, she had clean clothes on, and in the end that was my only priority—a foundational root around clothes!

I was the youngest of three children, and my brother and sister were several years older than I was. I was raised more like an only child; most of the rules they had to follow were no longer a priority for my parents by the time I came along. I can remember not having to eat everything on my dinner plate as long as it wasn't the meat portion of our dinner (my parents' foundational root around mealtime). For everything else, I could take one bite of and mush it around my plate, and my parents were content with my eating habits.

Having five children, you don't have the luxury of taking them out to dinner even to fast-food restaurants. It's expensive, everybody wants something different, and even when you decide on a place to eat, you have to deal with the looks from other patrons who are thinking, "Why would anyone want to take five children out to eat?" Thus, I became a pretty good cook, and I enjoyed it. In some ways it was therapeutic for me.

As every parent has to make a decision about their children's eating habits, I had to decide my priorities when it came to how much of and what my children had to eat. A great pediatrician once told me not to worry so much about my children's eating habits as about my own eating habits and the role model I am to my children. So my mealtime priorities consisted of just a few things: we all came to the table to eat together; if they didn't like what I cooked, then they could make something else (which didn't happen very often); and they could only put food on their plates that they would eat. These three mealtime priorities seemed to make mealtimes enjoyable for everyone. It worked for us, but every parent needs to make his or her own priorities, lay those foundational roots, and understand what causes unwarranted stress during mealtimes.

 "Parenthood has a very humanizing effect. Everything gets reduced to essentials."
—*Anonymous*

When my parents came to visit and I had a meeting to attend, my mother would make pot roast for our dinner. My mother was a good cook, but for some reason her pot roast was always dry and chewy. In one of the houses where we lived, there was a counter that could fit five bar stools. On the nights when my mom fixed pot roast, the children would sit at the counter in descending order, oldest to youngest, and when my mom wasn't looking they would all pass their pot roast down to Christine, who would feed it to our dog. Grandma's pot roast got to be a joke—she always thought they loved it, but it was the dog that loved pot roast night! And remember, that was my parents' priority—you always had to eat your meat.

The main point of this lesson is to understand what your priorities are as a parent and how they can make your life more or less complicated. Don't get so involved in life's duties that you forget the pleasures of having children. The items discussed above are in no way the most important priorities a parent has, but they are ones that cause lots of angst between parents and children. The sooner you understand what your priorities are, the better for your family and for you!

 "Don't be discouraged if your children reject your advice. Years later they will offer it to their own offspring." —Anonymous

Some priorities are more important and begin to surface as the child gets older. When my three older children entered high school, the Internet was becoming used much more commonly for social entertainment—a precursor to the social media sites now. At that time, I had only one computer, and it was on a desk in the kitchen area. My sons, Scott and Jeff, were chatting with some friends online when they both started laughing and (luckily) said, "Hey, Mom, look at this." I went over to the computer and on the screen saw a high school girl they knew—topless! Well, it didn't take me long to set my priorities about computer usage (even back then) and what was most important for the cyber safety of my family. My priority about computer usage was clearly explained to my children and enforced.

At the end of each lesson in this book, I will provide some Parent4Life helper activities that you may find useful. The first focuses on what your priorities are as a parent. Think about these and choose a topic that is causing you unnecessary stress. Then, using the chart below, see if this issue could be easily fixed once you define and understand your priorities. Once you do this, sit down with your children if they are old enough and communicate what your priorities are or aren't. Be consistent, and you will find that you have one less stressor. Remember, don't fret about everything; simplify your priorities so you don't drive yourself crazy!

Roots and Wings Helper Activity #1

Parenting items I need to prioritize so I don't drive myself crazy:	What are my priorities (my roots) around each item (let go of what's not critical)?
• *For example*: mealtime, school mornings, or bedtime	• Must take one bite of everything • Must have one vegetable at dinner

Parent4Life Lesson Two

Guilt—Don't Let It Get the Best of You

GUILT IS AN INTERESTING EMOTION that manifests itself in many different situations. It can be a negative, paralyzing emotion based on lack of acceptance of oneself or of one's situation. And it can be very destructive, especially to those trying to be effective parents. Many times when we feel guilty, we don't know what to do about it; that's the hardest part of guilt. It can very often contribute to a parent's lack of self-confidence. Guilt can also inhibit us from giving our children roots and wings.

If you are a parent or are in a parental role, I know you have felt guilty; it's part of the territory. We cannot completely rid ourselves of guilt, but we need to ask ourselves if this is guilt we deserve to be experiencing and, if so, what we can do about it. When Scott, Jeff, and Michelle were in middle school, I had an "aha" moment about guilt that provided me with a healthier perspective about being a parent. Most schools have an open-house night for parents, and theirs was no exception. I received a notice that the open house was scheduled for the following Tuesday night, and if a student's parent visited, the student would get one hundred extra-credit points. Well, this all sounded good, except that I had to go out of town the next week for work, and I was the only parent who could have attended. Of course my three children were devastated because extra points could make a grade difference at the end of the semester. The guilt hit me hard. But what could I do? I was scheduled to facilitate a three-day leadership course in Los Angeles and couldn't get out of the session. I also had three middle-school children mad at me. So I started thinking about options.

One skill for coping with guilt is what I call **changing or accepting**. Sometimes we have to accept a situation and let go of the guilt, but other times we can change the situation. That's what I set out to do: change the situation. I made an appointment with the principal and outlined the key points I wanted to discuss. In the meeting, I asked for him to explain the extra-point program and why the school felt it was necessary. He made a valid point that it was to increase parental participation. I proceeded to explain that it might be hurting the children of parents who wanted to be involved but who were unable to because of other circumstances. We came to a mutual agreement that he would allow parents who could not make the open-house night to schedule a one-on-one meeting with the teachers over the next thirty days. The children of those parents would still receive the one hundred extra-credit points. So that's what I did. My children were happy, the teachers were happy, and I didn't have to carry around the guilt about being a working parent. The next time you feel guilty, don't overlook the possibility of changing the situation. Most of the time there are alternatives.

There are several other "coping" skills I use for handling guilt:

Reflecting on motivation. An act done with positive intentions, especially without any self-interest, is not negative, even if it may harm others. In other words, sometimes we do something not meaning for or not knowing that it will negatively impact someone else. In several business settings, I have had to explain to employees that their current job roles and skill sets were not a match. Even though people can work on developing new skills, sometimes employees don't have the ability to grasp those needed skills. Working with other departments in the company, I try to find roles that are better matches with these employees' skill sets. Moving an employee to a new role can be done with positive intentions and seen as a win-win situation for everyone. Relating this to parenting, have you ever steered your children into or out of a sport or hobby that wasn't the best choice for them? I can remember my middle-school gym teacher telling me I probably shouldn't try out for the gymnastics team because I was so tall and because it would be challenging for me to compete with other girls who were much shorter than I was (I was five feet nine). The motivation of her comment was not meant to be hurtful, and she was trying to align my skill sets to something I could be more successful at (and she was right, gymnastics was not my sport). Sometimes it helps to reflect on the motivation in the situation. That motivation may be for the right reasons, and if that is the case, then let go of the guilt.

 "Before becoming a mother, I had a hundred theories on how to bring up children. Now I have seven children and only one theory: love them, especially when they least deserved to be loved." —Anonymous

Forgiving. Making mistakes is an inherent human quality. If you don't make mistakes, you are definitely not a normal human being. But if we are unable to forgive ourselves for our mistakes, we will never be able to properly forgive others. This is a hard one for me—forgiving myself. It goes back to my example in the introduction about the film *Sliding Doors*. I often catch myself thinking about the "if" and how much better a mother I might have been if my life path had been different. It's only been in the last few years that I have finally gotten to a place of peace and less guilt. I recently heard someone at a meeting going on and on about what his son and daughter were doing, what school they'd each been accepted to, etc. Now, it's OK for parents to brag about their children, but listening to these sorts of things from other parents can put me back into a place of guilt, and I don't like being there. Don't get me wrong, I am very proud of my five children and like to talk about them. However, I can remember being realistic when my children hit the high school years, thinking, "All I want is to get them through high school with no pregnancies, no drugs, and no jail time." And thankfully, it worked that way. We live in a society that pressures every child to be the best athlete, the best student, and the best of everything else. What a strain this puts on children, and what guilt it causes parents! As a parent, have realistic expectations of yourself and be able to forgive yourself for not being perfect.

Trying to find a work-life balance is not always easy, especially when you have children. I worked with a man, Enrique, who was very driven in his work but loved his family too. The company recognized his contributions and promoted him into a senior-level position. However, this new position required Enrique to move to a different city. This didn't sit well with his wife, who was comfortable with their home in Chicago and loved the things she could do with their two-year-old twin daughters. To ease his wife's pain, one of the first things Enrique did was to buy her the new Mercedes SUV she had wanted since the twins were born (sometimes bribery does work!). This made his wife happy, but she was still skeptical about the move. Enrique discussed his dilemma with me. Having already accepted the position, he now needed to make sure his family was as excited and as comfortable with the decision as he was. Enrique decided to take his wife and daughters on a house-hunting trip to the new city over the weekend. He had made some special preparations: welcome roses for his wife at the hotel, visits to great parks so the girls could play, and a special family dinner on Saturday night.

Thursday night before the early-morning Friday flight, Enrique made sure everything was packed (with twin two-year-olds, there's a lot of stuff). After he tucked his daughters into bed, Enrique opened a bottle of champagne and proposed a toast with his wife: "Here's to a new and exciting future—our future together." His wife was starting to come around, and there was even some excitement in her voice about the weekend trip.

Early Friday morning, Enrique finished packing the car and helped dress the twins. Traffic was light because it was so early, and they arrived at the airport in plenty of time. Enrique pulled up to the drop-off area to unload the luggage. He unfolded the twin stroller, buckled the girls in, and told his wife to go inside with the girls and get in line to check in. Enrique went back to the car, unloaded the multiple suitcases from the back, and put the suitcases on a luggage cart. Then he opened the car doors, took out the car seats, and added them to the cart. Luckily, he saw the diaper bag lying on the floor of the backseat, so he grabbed that too. He rolled the luggage cart inside and saw his wife going up to the counter. Enrique proceeded to the counter with all the travel gear. Just then one of the twins started crying. His wife picked her up, and Enrique provided the travel agent with the identification documents, and in turn the agent presented him with the tickets and gate information.

The luggage was checked, with the car seats nestled on the stroller, they headed to the gate. The plane was on time. Just before the security gate, the other twin started crying and throwing the well-known two-year-old tantrum. So Enrique picked her up, still pushing the stroller through the security line. Going through security was even better. It's so much fun when people are looking at you, thinking, "can't they control their kids?" Security made each of the girls walk through the scanner by themselves, with Enrique on one side and his wife on the other, coaxing them through. Enrique could start to see his wife's frustration, but he just gave her a big smile and mouthed, "I love you."

Through security and waiting to board, the girls quieted down, and things appeared calmer. Once on board, his wife took the aisle seat and buckled the twins into their car seats in the two seats next to her. Enrique sat directly across the aisle from his wife and said, "We made it." As the airplane took off down the runaway, his wife looked at him and asked what parking lot he parked her Mercedes in because it hadn't taken him long to park and get inside with the luggage cart. Enrique suddenly had a bad feeling in his stomach. "Honey," he said timidly, "I forgot to park the car. I was distracted, and I left it in the unloading area. I am so sorry!" Needless to say, she didn't talk to him for the rest of the flight, and the weekend didn't turn out like he'd planned. And yes, airport security towed and impounded her car. Work-life balance is so hard. It's more than OK to forgive yourself, especially when you try so hard!

One more skill for coping with guilt is to do a **reality check** with others. Sometimes we get so caught up with feeling guilty, we lose perspective. Talk to a friend, family member, or professional to see if your reasons for feeling guilty are truly valid. As I mentioned before, I majored in industrial and organizational psychology, and I needed to have a graduate degree in the field for my profession.

So, silly me, I decided to go to graduate school when my children were three, five, seven, seven, and nine. Needless to say, it was one of the hardest things I have ever done. I remember one semester in my second year of graduate school, I had a Thursday night class from six o'clock to ten o'clock. I had found a high-school student to watch the children on that night. She would arrive at five so I could get to class in plenty of time. One Thursday night, there was an exam in my class, and the sitter called to say she would be about fifteen minutes late. Well, that put me into a panic because my professor was not known for his kindness to those who were late to class. The sitter called me again and said she would be there by 5:30. At that time, Lisa was eleven so I made the decision to leave at 5:15 and put her in charge for fifteen minutes. No problem, right? The guilt started creeping in, but I had to leave, so off I went.

Meanwhile, my son Jeff, who was always very mechanically inclined and who is now an engineer, decided that his little sister, Christine, didn't need training wheels on her bike anymore. He got a wrench and proceeded to take off her training wheels. Jeff called Christine and told her to get on the now-two-wheeled bike and that he would help her. That was all fine until she went down the driveway, took a sharp curve, and fell on a sprinkler head, tearing open her right earlobe. As you can imagine, there was screaming and blood everywhere—just in time for the sitter to arrive at 5:35. As I pulled into the school parking lot, I got a frantic call from the sitter telling me I needed to come back home because Christine was bleeding everywhere. So I turned my car around, missed my test, and, six stitches later, I felt like the worst mother in the world! It took me a while to get over the guilt of that episode, but I had to have a reality check because I needed the graduate degree to further my ability to support my family. It was OK that I was going back to school, and some things happen even when you are there with your kids. But between you and me, I still feel a little guilty, and I thank God she wasn't hurt any worse.

I still deal with feelings of guilt today, but now it's about my grandchildren. Working full time doesn't lend itself to babysitting my grandchildren often, or much overnight babysitting. However, I do love spending a few of hours with them and almost every Sunday we try and get together for dinner, but rarely can I do extended stays at Grandma's house. I am sure the day will come when I will cherish those moments, but for now I just have to accept the situation and toss away the guilt of not being a "superwoman" grandmother.

Now it's your turn to think about the things that make you feel guilty in the parenting role. Be honest and open with yourself—it has a self-renewing effect, I promise.

Take a few minutes to write down the things that make you feel the guiltiest. After you do that, determine what you can do about that guilt. Remember, if we carry around too much guilt too much of the time, it hurts our self-esteem, affects our relationships, and can upset our health. And most importantly, it holds us back from providing roots and wings to our children.

Roots and Wings Helper Activity #2

What are the things that make me feel the guiltiest in the parental role?	Should I change the situation or just accept it?	How will I change the situation, or how will I let go of the guilt?	What guilt items do I need a reality check on?	What's the result of letting go of the guilt about the items listed? How should I feel?

Parent4Life Lesson Three

Understanding Discipline for You and Your Child

THERE HAVE BEEN SO MANY books written on discipline: on what works and what doesn't. I have read quite a few of them. I think one area that is continually missed is consideration for the personality of the child and an acknowledgment that what may work for one child won't always work for another. Don't get me wrong—there are some foundational rules that must be followed, but having five children, I can attest that it's not one size fits all. When it came to disciplining my children, it was by trial and error—mostly by error!

I can remember before I had children, I would see a child in the store throwing himself on the ground screaming, and I'd think that would *never* be my child. Wow, was I wrong. One of my first lessons happened when Lisa was about three and a half years old, Scott and Jeff were eighteen months old, and I was three months pregnant. We were at the neighborhood playground and Jeff did not want to go home, so I grabbed his hand and told him we were leaving. Well, Jeff lay on the ground and started screaming and kicking as I dragged him away from the playground. I didn't know what do except to think, "Please pass the salt so I can eat my words." After dragging Jeff about ten feet across the grass, I picked him up, still screaming and throwing a full-blown fit. Just when I had had enough of this behavior, Jeff's eyes rolled back in his head and he passed out. I became frantic and yelled at Lisa and Scott to run home with me so I could call 911 (cell phones were uncommon back then). A few seconds later, Jeff came to, quieter than before. Instead of calling 911, I called our pediatrician's office, and they said to bring him right in. After a thirty-minute wait and good money spent, I found out that I had a stubborn son who just held his breath while throwing a temper tantrum, and I was told to just let him pass out next time—no harm would come to him; he would take a breath when he needed to. So that's why I say each child is different. Years later, I understood that I could spank this child, and it might not faze him because he was so stubborn. I needed to allow Jeff to throw his fit in a safe environment, pass out, and then catch his breath. And like magic, it always worked! I had to change my perspective around discipline in order to provide Jeff the roots and wings he needed to grow.

When Lisa was thirteen, something else happened that changed my perspective that "my child would never do that." Lisa had asked her best friend, Jessica, to spend the night. Reluctantly I said yes; when I let one child have a friend sleep over, it usually meant that all the other siblings wanted a friend to stay overnight too (but that's another funny story). Lisa and Jessica spent most of the night in Lisa's bedroom talking and gossiping. I went in and told them good night around ten thirty. Around twelve thirty— yes, in the morning—I got a call from another parent, stating that my daughter and her friend were at their house "visiting" their son and asking if I could come and get them. Of course, my immediate response was, "It's not my daughter; there must be some mistake." Pleasantly she asked, "Are you Lisa's mom?" There was a moment of silence, and then I asked her to please wait a minute. I hurried into Lisa's room, and guess what—there was no Lisa or Jessica, and the window was open. I got back on the phone, asked where they lived, and said I would be there in fifteen minutes. Not only had Lisa and Jessica left the house and walked about one mile, they were two thirteen-year-old girls out alone at night—ugh! Of course, when I picked them up, they were quiet and apologetic, and Jessica begged me not to tell her parents. "Yeah, right," I said.

So, what does a parent do about discipline? I have come to the realization that this area is very individual, and each parent must make a decision and be very consistent with that decision. Discipline must follow the action and must be appropriate for the child's age. When it came to my son throwing a temper tantrum, the best solution was to put him in a safe environment and let him hold his breath. I know this might sound crazy, but it worked, and this behavior ceased over time. Sure, I would get "oh my God" looks and sneers from people watching, but we both made it through the situation. As for my thirteen-year-old daughter's decision to leave the house at midnight, I needed a consequence that would make her think about what could have happened. The best discipline I could think of at that time was taking away the phone that was in Lisa's room. It was a separate line from our home phone (at that time, I was the only one with a cell phone). This was devastating to a thirteen-year-old girl because now she had to go into the family room to talk, with four siblings listening to her every word. Also, her curfew for talking on the phone was now nine o'clock, the same as bedtime for her siblings. For me, the most difficult part of this consequence was not giving in for a month. But remember, consistency is one of the keys of discipline. Lisa was testing her wings, and I needed her to know what the boundaries were at that age.

I love the teenage years...just kidding! I guess with Lisa coming into her teens first, I have lots of stories about her in particular. I didn't know what to expect, and all I could do was take it one day at a time. As I mentioned above, cell phones were around then, but this was at the time when only Mom had one. Lisa having her own landline in her room with her own phone number—that was a big deal! Lisa was a good daughter, and I guess I should have known that she would want to talk on the phone after ten o'clock, which was her normal phone curfew time. Several nights, after I fell asleep, I woke to a whispered conversation and quiet giggling. When I looked at the clock, I discovered it was eleven o'clock or midnight, well past curfew. Like most rational parents, I politely reminded Lisa about her phone curfew and waited for her to end the conversation (which was with a boy, I was sure). After about two weeks of this off and on, I awoke once again to soft chatter from down the hall. Hopping out of bed with my anger level rising, I didn't take my own advice and think about what I should do. Instead I quickly walked down the hall, opened Lisa's door, and found her lying on her bed with an "oh no" expression on her face. I went over to the wall where the phone jack was, and instead of just unplugging the phone and taking it out of her room, I let my emotions get the best of me and ripped the cord from the wall, leaving some exposed wires. Then I turned to Lisa and said, "Well, guess your conversation is over, now and in the future." I don't know who was more surprised, she or I, or her siblings when they saw the dangling cords in the morning. The lesson here is that we parents are not perfect, and it is so important not to discipline a child in anger. Because I let my emotions get the better of me, it cost me about fifty dollars to repair the phone jack when I could have just unplugged it and taken the phone from her room. Anger can be costly in many ways, so be careful!

Here's another funny-but-effective story on discipline. My kids wanted a dog, so of course, when one of them found a cute puppy wandering the streets, they brought her home and she became our dog. Sound familiar? We named the dog Shadow because she was all black except for a small white patch on her chest. Shadow was a medium-sized dog, probably a mix between a Collie and a Lab. She spent most of her day in the backyard while we were at school and work. I made a deal with my sons that we could keep her if they picked up the dog poop in the backyard. Eagerly, they both agreed, and it worked well for the first month. Then the newness of the dog wore off, and cleanup became a struggle. We lived in sunny San Diego, which meant the kids were outside playing all the time, and it was warm, so having dog poop around was not a good thing.

Learning from what I'd done with Lisa and her phone, I decided to try something a little different (and smarter). I sat my sons down and explained the expectation: twice a week, the dog poop would need to be picked up. I even gave them the option of picking which days were best for them, and since there were two of them, they each only had to do one day a week. They chose Tuesday and Saturday as the days. The first week was great, and there were no problems. The second week, Scott got Jeff to take his day; the third week, Scott and Jeff argued about who had what day. One month into this—disaster. I reminded each son of my expectations and that there would be a consequence if the chore was not done.

The next Tuesday came and went with no dog poop picked up. On Wednesday I got four plastic grocery bags and put one inside the other to make two leak-proof bags. I proceeded to go out in the backyard and put the piles of dog poop into the plastic grocery bags. That's not as bad as it seems—about three piles of dog poop in each bag. I carefully placed the bags on each boy's bed. The lesson was about to begin. My sons came home from school, and upon entering their bedroom, they smelled something. I heard them yell, "Oh, *gross—Mommm!*" I walked into their room, reminded them of our agreement, and stated that they had not kept their ends of the bargain. In addition, I told them that if I had to pick the poop up again, the same thing would happen. They shook their heads in complete dismay at what I had done.

Saturday came with soccer games, a birthday party to go to, and friends spending the night. Guess what didn't get done. I didn't say anything on Sunday; I just waited. Nothing happened. On Monday morning the children left for school, and before I got ready for work, I quickly went out and put the dog poop into two bags again—I even had some stinky, runny poop this time! I wasn't there when my sons came home from school, but my daughters couldn't wait to tell me what happened when the boys walked into their fragrant rooms. You guessed it: problem solved. They picked up the poop from then on, and life was good. It goes to show that this kind of discipline—natural consequences and consistent follow-through—can be very effective. It doesn't work all the time, but looking at the situation and evaluating the best way to deal with it helps a lot.

Reflecting on my many experiences at work, I remember facilitating a team-building session in which I asked each participant to think about words of wisdom that had an impact on their lives. This was a very moving experience and spoke volumes about how the participants were raised and how they experienced their lives growing up. One of the best pieces of advice given that day was by a woman who told us that when she was growing up, her parents had a plaque above their front door that read, "Return with Honor." What a great way for children to learn about accountability from their parents—a reinforcement of a family value. A subtle-but-powerful way to embed roots and provide wings for their children. I wish I had heard about this years ago! What advice or saying has had a meaningful impact on you? Write it down. Why has it impacted you, and what does it look like when it's acted on? Have you shared this with your children, or will you when they get older?

It was a big deal for me to go grocery shopping with five children, especially when they were very small. Picture this: I had Christine in a front pack, Michelle sitting in the cart, and Lisa trying desperately to hold on to Scott's and Jeff's hands. Store patrons thought I was crazy! One day, Scott and Jeff decided to tease Michelle as she sat in the cart. Both of them stood on the front rail at the base of the cart, with their hands on the cart handle. This made the cart unbalanced, so it started falling toward them. They jumped off, and poor Michelle went crashing to the floor, where her knees got trapped under the front of the basket. Michelle let out an agonized cry that every mother knows. I carefully picked her and the basket up off the floor, although I didn't know if her poor little legs were broken. The store manager suggested he call for medical help, but I decided to just take her to the local emergency room. Luckily, her young bones were still soft, and there was no damage except some bruising.

It was at that point I decided that I needed additional help, so I asked my grandmother to help me go grocery shopping. Even at eighty years old, she was in good condition and up for the challenge. I would pick her up every Friday, in the late afternoon, and off to the grocery store we would go to get food for the entire next week. At that time, one of my discipline beliefs was that I would not let my children open crackers or any other food while we were in the store, and I had kept this rule consistent. I told my grandmother that this was my rule, and she agreed to abide by it. Then, on a subsequent shopping trip, Christine was teething, and the other four were pushing my buttons. The checkout line was long because it was late Friday afternoon, and everyone else was there getting weekend supplies. My grandmother suggested she take some of the children to the car while I waited in line, but being Supermom, I said it was OK, and they could just wait. Michelle started to cry because she wanted out of the basket, and the boys were teasing Lisa, another one of their favorite pastimes. As the whining started to get louder, and more disgusted looks came my way, I was completely frazzled. I decided to open the bag of animal crackers and let the children who were quiet get a handful. When I had everyone's attention, their hands were out, and the whining had stopped, I passed out the animal crackers. My grandmother said, "I thought you told me not to do that. I would have done that a long time ago." You can guess what came next: "I'm thirsty." So I opened the juice packets. The children were happy and quiet, but I was extremely mad at myself. And that wasn't the worst part of it—it was the precedent I set. Because guess what happened at the next grocery store visit. I opened up the animal crackers, the string cheese, and whatever else they wanted! Yes, consistency is the key to discipline. You may say to yourself, "That it is not a big deal; I give my kids food at the store all the time." And it's true: it's not that big of a deal. However, it made me realize that I wasn't consistent in other areas of discipline as well, and to be most effective, I couldn't give in one time and not the next time.

As I mentioned earlier, discipline must be defined by each parent and made a part of the family value system. Easier said than done. Too often we parents react to the immediate situation out of anger or frustration—not the best model for discipline. Someone once asked me if I could discipline without yelling. I had never really thought about it, but what a great question. I reflected about this every time I disciplined my children. Unfortunately, I yelled a lot. More importantly, I found that I could not discipline all of my children in the exact same way, which presented even more of a challenge. Remember earlier in this chapter when I discussed how stubborn my son Jeff was? Each of my five children had very different personalities and I needed different methods of discipline to be effective as a parent in giving them roots and wings. Of course, I had my threshold of what was acceptable and what was not. But I wish I had known then what I know now. It would have made my life and my children's lives much less stressful. If someone had asked me a few simple but probing questions, I might have consciously chosen a better path to discipline. If you're finding this a challenge too, don't feel too bad. Even a doctor of human behavior struggled with this one.

 "Live so that when your children think of fairness and integrity, they think of you." —Anonymous

Take a few minutes to complete the activity below. Think about what really works when you discipline your own children and what doesn't work as well, and ask yourself why. By answering these questions, it will help you and your children understand where the boundaries are and where they can test their wings.

Roots and Wings Helper Activity #3

Making discipline easier for you—honestly answer a few simple but important questions:

1. What are the top three values you live by? (This is usually a very hard question to answer.)
 	
    •
    •
    •

2. What are your beliefs about discipline for your children?
3. Why are these your beliefs? Was it how you were raised or something you have read?
4. How effective are your methods of discipline? What is working and what is not working?

5. Rate yourself on the consistency of your discipline. It is important for you and your child that you set clear boundaries and expectations.
 	
    1 Not consistent at all
    2 Once in a while I show consistency
    3 Almost always consistent
    4 Always consistent

6. What steps can I take to make discipline easier for me and my children?

Parent4Life Lesson Four

Extension of You, but Not *You*!

I NEVER THOUGHT ANY OF my five children looked much like me, and I was OK with that, but what I did expect was that they would all have my personality (go ahead, it's OK to laugh!). I would describe my personality as having the following positive traits: early riser, organized, ambitious, athletic, works easily through conflict—my list of good traits goes on (remember, this is my perception!). I could see that my children were all different, but it hit me between the eyes when one of my daughters said to me, "Mom, I am not you!" It was another "aha" moment that shook my world as a parent. (Funny, I seem to have lots of those moments.) She was right; she and her siblings were not me. Each of them had a personality different from mine and different from each other—wow! Even my twin sons have different personalities—can you imagine that?

You may be asking, "So what?" To illustrate, let's take a Saturday morning in my home when my children were growing up. I would get up early, make my to-do list, pick up around the house, or do some yard work. A few of the children liked to sleep late or just hang out in their rooms, relaxing. In my world, when you have chores to do, they must be done by midmorning—that was how my parents raised me. But because of my children's personality differences, I had to rethink the situation and allow the chores to get done in their timeframes. As long as the chores were done by sundown, who cared, right? Well, I did! It took me a long time to be OK with that one difference in behavior, but I was causing myself undue stress just because my personality was different from any of my five children. I was trying to provide my children roots and wings, but this added an unexpected twist to my thinking. I had to question myself on where I needed to let go of my parents' foundations and create new ones with my own children.

Too often I see parents living vicariously through their children. I'm not saying that parents can't gently nudge a child to play a sport or take dance lessons, but the child's personality begins to be shaped more like the parent's than the child's real self. Even today, if I go over to my daughter's home (won't say which daughter) and I see clothes in the dryer not folded, it drives me crazy. But she works and takes care of my grandchildren, and when she is ready to fold the clothes, she'll do it, and the clothes will be fine—wrinkled, but placing much less stress on her.

Once we understand that our children have personalities different from our own, one of our most important roles as parents is to help shape those personalities by building self-esteem. This is one way we can promote and cultivate children's individuality and help create roots and wings. If I had to raise my children all over again, I'd build self-esteem first and the house later. I'd finger-paint more and point the finger less. I'd do more hugging and less tugging. These are choices that shape children's self-esteem and provide strong wings when they are ready to fly.

"A parent is a person who shows you the light when you just see the dark." —Anonymous

Children's self-esteem is influenced so much by those around them. Healthy self-esteem is a child's armor against the world. For those of us who have an impact on a child's life, we should hold the building of a child's self-esteem very close to our hearts and minds. Don't mess this up—the scars can last a lifetime.

Self-esteem refers to feelings of capability combined with feelings of love, and patterns of self-esteem start early in life. For example, when a baby reaches a new milestone like crawling or walking, he feels a sense of confidence. A baby who takes that first walk across the room not only feels competent but also receives reinforcement from everyone who is watching. Self-esteem also relates to the feeling of being loved. A child who has accomplished a milestone but does not feel loved will soon experience low self-esteem. I have no funny stories on this topic. I have seen too many times in my professional career how low self-esteem can negatively impact a person's life into adulthood.

One of the worst things I've heard a parent say to a child is, "You're so stupid." The immediate and long-term effects of those words are amazing. In my professional work with organizations, I often ask my session participants, "What is the worst feedback you have ever gotten in your professional or personal life?" You would be surprised how many times I hear people answer that it was when a mom, dad, caregiver, or teacher called them stupid or worthless.

For example, in a professional setting, I once mentored a woman who had always had a weight problem, and because of her low self-esteem, she had never thought about moving beyond her current position. I had spent several mentoring sessions with her when I finally asked what was holding her back from wanting more in her career. Tears welled up in her eyes, and she said quietly, "My mom told me how fat and stupid I was growing up." I worked with her and got her to realize all the awesome things she had accomplished and what the possibilities were for the future. That Fall semester, she enrolled in college, and several years later she finished her degree. Although she accomplished this later in life, it was a very important milestone. Fortunately, her mom came to her graduation, and she finally received the recognition and self-esteem booster she had so desperately needed years earlier.

The story above may be an extreme example, but think about what you say to your children. If you are a parent or grandparent, coach or other parental figure, are you building up or tearing down the self-esteem of children in your care? I hate it when someone calls a child, a friend, or a family member stupid, and for that reason I forbade my own children from calling each other stupid (this was one of my priorities). Research suggests that children with low self-esteem will find challenges to be sources of anxiety and may become passive, withdrawn, or depressed. Faced with something new, their immediate responses are usually, "I can't." Remember, it's not just words that are destructive; its withholding acknowledgement, not being patient, or not taking the time to show a child how to do something, coaching him or her along the way.

Children with healthy self-esteem are comfortable with new things and new settings. They have a sense of optimism that prevails even when they fail at something. For example, my son Jeff was an awesome soccer goalie. It wasn't just me who thought so—it was everyone on his team. When Jeff was eleven years old, he was in a championship soccer tournament. His twin brother, Scott, a forward, and Jeff, the goalie, were a dynamic duo, determined to win the tournament. In the final championship game, the score was tied 2–2, with about one minute left to play, when a forward on the opponent's team came out of nowhere through our defenders, dribbled down the field, and set up for the winning goal between the opponent and Jeff. Nobody thought the opponent would score, but a quick kick to the right corner caught Jeff off guard, and the other team scored the winning goal. Jeff put his head down and grabbed the side of the goalpost. My heart sank, and I wanted to run out immediately and hug him, but I knew that would embarrass him. After a few minutes, the coach walked onto the field, put his arm around Jeff, and comforted him. I didn't know what he said at the time, but I did know it would be words of praise, not of anger or disappointment.

Later I asked the coach what he'd said. He had told Jeff that this was a team sport, and the opponent went past ten other team members before he got to Jeff—and nobody stopped him. He also told Jeff there was not another goalie he would rather have on his team, and that meant a lot because this was a competitive club soccer in Southern California. It's moments like these that build a child's self-esteem. Take careful notice of what you say to any child. His or her self-esteem is fragile and needs TLC. All children need a little help, a little hope, and somebody who believes in them. There's nothing that will build stronger roots and wings in children than that.

So what can we all do to build a child's self-esteem? Once again, it's not rocket science, but we must keep it at the front of our minds and constantly reinforce it with everything that comes into and out of our children's lives. Think of these tips as a guide to a lifelong investment in your child.

Parent4Life Tips

1. Watch what you say! Children are very sensitive to the words of a parent, grandparent, teacher, or caregiver. What might be a joke to you may not be funny to the child. He or she will internalize the comment, and it will pick away at the child's self-esteem, especially if the comment is repeated or said in anger.
2. Identify and redirect your children's inaccurate beliefs about themselves. Helping children acquire more accurate perceptions will distinguish false beliefs from true ones (unless those false beliefs are reinforced).
3. Too often I hear a child state, "I am not good at anything." The parent or caregiver must be a positive role model. If you set too many limitations on yourself, your child will eventually mirror what you are saying and replicate your behaviors. Nurture your own self-esteem, and your children will have a great role model.

When I started graduate school, I was really concerned about whether I would make it through the program. But even though I was scared, I always said to myself, "I can do it." I had to take each semester one at a time because facing four years of work before I'd get my doctorate was overwhelming. In my third year, the head of the program wrote me a note thanking me for my "can do" attitude on a project I completed for him. I didn't fully realize the effect this had on my children until my daughter Lisa, as an adult, decided to go back to school for her nursing degree, despite having a six-month-old baby and a relationship that was unraveling. She said to me, "Mom, if you made it with five of us, I can do it too!" Wow, the impact of what we say and do as parents—don't ever underestimate it.

I emphasize self-esteem because it can be the foundation of success and failure. I don't mean financial success; I am talking about living each day with happiness and confidence in who you are and what you can do. Be a positive role model and nurture your own self-esteem along with your children's. I used my wings to go back to school, and so did my daughter.

Another way to be a positive role model to your children is to react appropriately to objections they may have about some aspect of themselves. For example, my daughter Michelle once told me that she did not like her name and wished she had been called something else. I could have said, "Yes, you're right, I don't really like the name either," but that was not true. What I wanted her to know was that I loved the name Michelle, and I also gave her my own middle name. In addition, her initials are the same as my mother's. All of those things make her name special to me. When my youngest child was born, I wanted to name her Christine because it meant "Christian," and she would be my final child blessing. It is normal for children not to like something about themselves, such as their names or heights, but it's what a parent does with those objections that will make a lifetime of difference.

 "It was my mother who taught us to stand up to our problems, not only in the world around us but in ourselves." —Dorothy Hughes

Parents should also be sure not to underestimate each child's unique characteristics. There is a cardinal rule that one should not compare a child with another sibling or somebody else's child. Have you ever heard a parent say, "I wish my child was more like yours," underestimating each child's unique characteristics? We may think it is funny, but have you ever heard someone call themselves the "bad seed" of the family? Being told you're the bad seed of the family can easily be adopted by the child in behavioral terms. This can become a negative self-fulfilling prophecy. As parents, we must love and respect each child. Deep roots begin with loving our children for who they are, not who we want them to be, which can sometimes be very difficult for parents.

Now What about You?

I have talked a lot about raising children and being that positive influence that gives them roots and wings. But it wasn't until my children were much older that it occurred to me to think about my own personality and idiosyncrasies. Who am I, and how does that impact my relationship with my children? I spent a total of eight years in college studying human behavior, yet I never thought to consider how my personality impacted each of my children. My graduate school professors would be shaking their heads. The cliché about the cobbler's children without shoes must be relevant here! The psychologist analyzing human behavior but not her own—now that's funny! You can avoid my mistake by spending a few minutes now thinking about your own personality. How does it positively blend with your children, and where does it clash? Changing your behavior or adjusting your personality is very difficult, but sometimes it's necessary in the parental role to be successful.

One challenge I faced with my personality was with expressing verbal love to my children. Years ago I thought that if I showed my children love, then I didn't need to tell them I loved them. Deep down inside, it was hard for me to say those words even though I loved my children more than life itself. It took a crisis situation with one of my daughters and her telling me that she needed to hear those words for the lesson to finally sink into my heart and mind. I realized then how very important it was to say, "I love you." Changing my behavior was difficult, but I made it a point to tell all my children almost daily that I loved them. Fast-forward to today, and it's just something we say to each other. It's routine, but the meaning has never lessened. When my grandson Nick was about four, I would kiss him and tell him how much I loved him and that Grandma's kisses would always be with him. He just laughed as he rubbed his cheek. Little did he know how true it was. I showed him love, but I wanted him to hear it too. I want all my grandchildren to know I love them and hear those words continuously from me. Don't ever underestimate the importance of telling your children that you love them

It has become so routine for me to end my phone conversations with my children or grandchildren by saying, "I love you" that sometimes at work I end a conversation with a coworker in the same way. Then I have to apologize profusely and tell them I just ended a phone call with a family member, and it's just something we say to each other. There is usually dead silence on the phone while the person is embarrassed for me, or sometimes they say nothing and hang up. I have no regrets, however, because I worked very hard to change my behavior and tell my children verbally that I loved them. It's something that was important to me and to them! Stop and think about how often you say those words to your children. It's very easy when they are babies, but it can get harder as they get older. I know I did not say those words enough when I was raising my children.

Strengths and Weaknesses

Most likely, sometime in your life you have been asked to think about what your strengths and weaknesses are. In the business world, we assess employees formally and informally in these two areas many times in their careers. This not only helps a company understand their talents and skills, but it also provides targeted development opportunities to help employees achieve career growth. When I am coaching employees, they often get stuck on their weaknesses. It's such a part of human nature that we gravitate to negative areas first. But I quickly remind them that their strengths are what have made them successful, so we shouldn't only concentrate on the improvement opportunities. We should always have a nice balance between the two spectrums. Children who know their strengths have the wings to explore life. And when parents understand their own strengths and weaknesses, it allows for complete transparency, which continues to build deep roots and widespread wings in their children. When a parent allows their child to see the parent's strengths and areas that make them vulnerable it teaches a child that no one is perfect. Children see and understand that even their parents have strengths and weaknesses and can use them to navigate life successfully.

As parents, we must be able to recognize and accept our strengths and weaknesses. Very much like in business, try to discover what you're really good at and what you need help with. Some of your strengths may help build strong roots and wings for your children, while your weaknesses may hamper your ability do this. Once you understand and recognize these areas, ask yourself when and where your strengths and weaknesses show up when dealing with your children and in what situations.

This type of analysis is common in psychology, which is a fascinating subject to me—trying to understand, explain, and predict behavior. During my doctoral program, I took many personality assessments, and nearly all of the time I thought, "Wow, these results sound just like me." If you take these kinds of assessments honestly, the results should be accurate and informative. But when something comes back that you don't like, doubt sets in about whether this is really you or not. After I took several assessments and began analyzing my behavior as a parent, some common themes surfaced.

 "I am a mother myself, so why did it take me thirty years to understand that mothers aren't perfect?" —Anonymous

One of my strengths, not only as a parent but also in my work life, is that I am a great multi-tasker. I can do multiple jobs at once—I guess you could say that I can juggle all the balls in the air most of the time and do a pretty good job of it. Another strength I have is being organized. These two strengths have provided me the opportunity of being a mother, a student, and an employee all at once. This is not to say that other people couldn't do the same with different strengths, but these are my natural strengths that have helped me throughout my life. With these, I hope I have role modeled to my children how to do multiple things in a somewhat-structured way. Whether it fit their personalities was a different concern; as I explained above, each child has a different personality. What was most important is that I recognized my strengths and used them to hopefully help our family unit in times that were very hectic and stressful. I wanted my children to learn what their natural strengths were and how they could use them throughout their own lives.

So what are my areas for improvement? I have many, but a specific area for development is that I am controlling. Yes, with my family—and also sometimes at work. Now, that isn't all bad, but there are times when I hampered the opportunity to let my children grow their wings. Most parents are protective, but I have taken it to extremes because of my controlling behavior.

This is an embarrassing example of what not to do if being controlling is one of your weaknesses like it is mine. When my sons were freshman in high school, they played on the varsity soccer team. Now, my twin sons were not small at that age, but the junior and senior boys were much larger in height and weight. We had traveled to another high school for a night game, and, of course, I had to sit in the first row of the bleachers along with my three daughters. The game was unusually rough, and close to the end of it I could feel myself starting to become the controlling mom monster. I yelled at the referees and was not being a very good role model for my daughters. The final whistle blew, and the game ended with our team winning. My son Jeff, the goalie, was still on the field pulling off his goalie gloves and shirt when two boys from the other team started to harass him (that is my word, not his). The conversation appeared to be esclating, so, giving in to my overly controlling behavior, I leaped over the metal bannister and ran onto the field between my son and the other two boys. I told them to get off the field, that the game was over, and to leave my son alone. Well, you can guess how embarrassed my son was, and I even embarrassed myself that time. And that was not the worst part—after I jumped over the rail, so did my oldest daughter, Lisa, concerned about her brothers and probably about me! I learned that day that my controlling behavior had its limits, and I needed to learn them. I was not helping my children grow roots or wings; rather, I was showing them what a fool their mother was.

I needed to examine how to change this controlling behavior and let go of some things, especially when it involved my children. I did an exercise similar to the one at the end of this lesson and slowly started to change this weakness into something that was manageable. Remember, we all have strengths that can be leveraged for our success in a job, at school, or while raising a child. It's important that you know both your strengths and weaknessess, and how they can and will impact your parenting style.

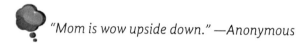 *"Mom is wow upside down." —Anonymous*

When working with companies, I frequently refer to the "shadow" of the leader. Each time I conduct leadership sessions, I emphasize that all leaders, whether it's the executive leader or the front-line leader, have a shadow that falls on the people who they come into contact with both inside and outside the company. I think the same thing is true for those in the parental role. The interactions we have with our children all cast a shadow. The size and shape of this shadow is determined by our own strengths and weaknesses as a parent. We can adjust and modify this shadow as needed as long as we understand who we are and are willing to change for our children's well-being. As I tell leaders, it's up to them to adjust their shadows and be the best possible leaders they can be. The same is true for parents—it's up to us to adjust our parenting styles as needed.

I think it's important that each of us knows our personal strengths and weaknesses, whether in work, in personal relationships, or in raising children. If I am controlling, but I use this quality to guide my children in growing deep roots, then I am using it appropriately. But too much of a strength can become a weakness. If I controlled my children's every moment, I could not provide them with the opportunity to grow their wings. Have you taken time to really think about what your strengths and weaknesses are in the parent role?

Roots and Wings Helper Activity #4

Take a few minutes to write down the strengths and weaknesses that might help or hinder your ability as a parent or caregiver to give your children roots and wings.

What are my strengths?	How can I leverage my strengths to give my children roots and wings?	What are my weaknesses?	How can I improve my weaknesses?

Once you have finished this exercise, ask your spouse, partner, or a trusted friend for feedback. Is this an accurate self-perception, or are there other things that should be on the list? Are there things that should be removed from the list? Being a parent or being in a parental role is not easy, and it's OK to ask for help. We can't always be supermoms or superdads, and that is OK. We just need to be the best role models we can be. Doing this speaks louder than any words ever could.

Conclusion

Back to the Beginning—Roots and Wings

SEVERAL DIPLOMAS HANG IN MY office: my bachelor's, my master's, and my doctoral degree. They look impressive to some. But the most important items I have in my office are displayed proudly on my desk: the pictures of my five children and my grandchildren. I can honestly say the eight years of college were much easier than raising my kids. In almost every profession, you have to get certified or pass some kind of test before you take the job. Isn't it interesting that you can become a parent with no training? I believe it is one of the most challenging jobs you will ever have, but it will also be the most rewarding one in so many ways.

 "Though parenthood is the most important of all professions, requiring more knowledge than any other department in human affairs, there is no attention given to preparation for this office." —Elizabeth Cady Stanton

As guardians of our children, we have an enormous responsibility. Those of us who influence children need to remember that they have certain basic needs. Psychologist Abraham Maslow's well-known hierarchy of needs begins with food and shelter. Everything in this book is extremely valuable in helping raise a productive, well-balanced child, but if that child doesn't have the basics, not much else matters. There are too many children who are hungry at home or who may have no home at all. I once visited a food bank that delivered snacks to city schools so the children would have something to eat over the weekend. There are more children whose basic needs are unmet than you might think, and each of us has a responsibility to make sure those children get what they need. Get involved where you live; donate your time or money to worthy causes that help parents get educated and find employment so they can provide for their children's basic needs. Get your children involved too. Volunteer together at a food bank or somewhere you and your child will get exposure to things you don't always see and frankly probably don't want to think about. I am blessed that my five children never went hungry (and neither did our dog, thanks to Grandma's roast). All of us have a responsibility to children. Don't assume that someone else will take care of needy kids. Take the responsibility seriously and start today.

At the beginning of this book, I told you that I was in the midst of fighting cancer when I first started thinking about my role as a parent and giving my children roots and wings. As I looked around the chemo lab, I had a profound experience in thinking about each of the patients. We all came from different backgrounds and experiences, but we all had one common goal: to beat cancer! I often think about those of us who have a parenting role in a similar way. We too have a common goal, which is supporting our children, giving them the love necessary to grow deep roots, and providing them with the necessary freedoms to spread their wings and explore. Let's not get so caught up in the ritual do's and don'ts of raising children. Keep your arms open when your children need a hug. Have an understanding heart when they need a friend. Sometimes your gentle eyes need to be stern when children need a lesson. Use your strength and love to guide them and give them the wings to fly.

I believe in and live the concept of roots and wings. Think about the roots you are developing for your children. How deep are these roots, and are their wings strong enough to withstand the wind? As I look at my five adult children, sure, there are things I wish I had done differently (remember the guilt chapter?), and I wish I had known then what I know today. But that's unrealistic, and I am finally OK with that. Plant the roots deep, and when the time comes for giving your children wings, it will become much easier, I promise.

 "There is no way to be a perfect parent and a million ways to be a good parent." —Anonymous

Looking back at my childrearing years, I have an array of emotions, as most parents do. If I knew then what I know today, things could have been easier on all of us. Take the time to prioritize what's most important to you in raising your children. Don't make everything so complicated that you don't have the time, effort, or patience to enjoy them. Understand the priorities (roots) that are individual to your parenting style. Don't fuss over every little thing. It's true—"Don't sweat the small stuff." Make life simpler by understanding what is most important to you, what can you live with, and, most importantly, what you can let go of!

Don't let your guilt get the best of you. Decide what you can do with things that overwhelm you with guilt, understand them, acknowledge them, and then do something about them! Think about the values you live by. Could a stranger see evidence of those values in your behavior as a parent?

Remember that discipline is unique to your parenting style and can be unique for each child. What works for one child may not work for another. Form foundational disciplining guidelines and be consistent. Share those guidelines and consequences with your children. Revisit them as your children get older, and don't discipline in anger. Let your discipline guidelines be your own, not simply the ones you were raised with or that you read about somewhere. It's important to find out what works best for you and your family.

As a parent, you mold your children's self-esteem. Ask yourself what that will look like in five, ten, fifteen, and twenty years from now. Never underestimate the impact you can have on your children's confidence and ability to function in the future. Be that positive role model. Parenting is an awesome gift; be wise with it.

 "Before you were conceived I wanted you. Before you were born I loved you. Before you were an hour old I would die for you. That is the miracle of life." —Anonymous

I hope some of the thoughts I have shared in this book made you laugh and, more importantly, will help you navigate parenthood. Every person who has some influence in a child's life has an enormous responsibility. Don't ever underestimate the impact you can and do have. Being a parent enables you to influence the future!

When I do professional coaching, I know the biggest hurdle will come when the session is over. The clients leave motivated and excited about their development, and the commitment level is high. But when a couple of days or weeks go by, they get caught up in the everyday whirlwind and no longer have time to work on their development. It takes real dedication to make time for personal development. I challenge you to take parent time for yourself. Do some of the activities in this book and post the results somewhere you can see them every day. Challenge yourself to change your behavior. Remember, it takes days of repeating a new behavior before it becomes a routine. Ask for help; it's OK. This was another one of my biggest "aha" moments—I didn't have to be a parent all by myself (once I admitted that I wasn't a supermom!). Engage your spouse, a friend, or a local support group. Not only will you find out that other parents experience the same things, but this will hold you accountable to make needed changes.

Fortunately or unfortunately, I have experienced a lot of life-changing events. Having five children very close together, being a single parent, having cancer, getting my doctorate—all of these have had a major impact on me. Most of you have had life-changing events too, and some of you have had even more to deal with. Don't be like me, waiting until I was diagnosed with cancer to think about my role as a parent. Do it today. Make life easier. Understand what's important to you in raising your children. Let go of your guilt. Be proactive, not reactive. And most importantly, give your children roots and wings.

I loved writing this book, and I hope you have enjoyed and learned something from it too. Being a parent or having some influence on a child's life brings much joy, but it can also bring exhaustion and sadness. Nothing else will make you as happy or as sad, as proud or as tired, for nothing is quite as hard as helping a child develop his or her own individuality, especially while you struggle to keep your own. The guidelines can be simple for giving your children roots and wings: love, limit, and let them be who they are.

I invite you to visit my website, www.Parent4Life.com, where I offer some additional tips and resources. More importantly, I would love to hear your Parent4Life tips! Parenting is our hardest job, so let us share, laugh, and enjoy each other's experiences. I look forward to hearing from you soon!

About the Author

DR. LAURA L. FREEMAN IS the mother of five children and has worked as an industrial and organizational psychologist with several Fortune 500 companies in her career. Her passion for helping people succeed both personally and professionally has always been a cornerstone to the many roles she has had. Dr. Laura has worked with and coached many adults whose lives were positively and negatively impacted in childhood. She firmly believes that children require guidance and love far more than instruction. She considers parenthood to be by far the most important, impactful, and hardest job a person will ever have. Dr. Laura believes the greatest gifts we can give our children are roots and wings, something she continually teaches to herself and to her readers.

Made in the USA
San Bernardino, CA
10 May 2015